Playing Alice

Jenny Hamlett

Indigo Dreams Publishing

First Edition: Playing Alice
First published in Great Britain in 2017 by:
Indigo Dreams Publishing Ltd
24 Forest Houses
Halwill
Beaworthy
EX21 5UU
www.indigodreams.co.uk

ISBN 978-1-910834-32-9

British Library Cataloguing in Publication Data. A CIP record for this book can be obtained from the British Library.

Designed and typeset in Palatino Linotype by Indigo Dreams.
Printed and bound in Great Britain by 4Edge Ltd
www.4edge.co.uk

Cover design by Ronnie Goodyer

Papers used by Indigo Dreams are recyclable products made from wood grown in sustainable forests following the guidance of the Forest Stewardship Council.

for Evie when she is grown

Acknowledgements

Acumen, Artemis, The Broadsheet, The Interpreter's House, Orbis, South, Reach Poetry and Sarasvati magazines.

Moor Poets Volume III, Cornwall – An Anthology of Poetry and Photographs, Openings – An Anthology by Open University Poets, and Fanfare – Poems by Contemporary Women Poets

The app – Words in Air

Poems short listed in competitions: *On Loch Bá* in Poems on the Move and published on the buses in Guernsey, *Whitehorse Hill Burial* in Second Light.

Thank you to my husband Ian for his proof reading and to Alice Kavournas for her initial in-depth reading of forty poems. Thank you to all my poetry groups in Cornwall and Devon for their help with individual poems and a very special thank you to Zeeba Ansari for her patient and detailed reading of the poems and for her guidance with the whole collection.

Also by Jenny Hamlett:

Talisman (IDP)
Watching the Sea Four Ways (The Frogmore Press)
Ring Three Times for the Kitchen Maid (Palores)

CONTENTS

If Centuries Were Seconds

Going In

Winter Pass

Saying Goodbye

Playing Alice

If Centuries Were Seconds

Yorkshire Dales
Drovers Road since
before Roman times

Mastiles Lane
Kilnsey to Malham

The track is silent
listening for lost footsteps …

once lay brothers watched
huge flocks on the open moor

alert for the crow pecking
at new-born lambs' eyes,

alert for the fox, for winter storms
and sensing the first scent of snow.

What did they think – bowed in work
while the monks prayed

and the abbey grew rich?
Only the wind answers,

beating across the springy turf,
hurling itself round a limestone cliff.

Midsummer. They counted Swaledales,
* *Yan, tan, tether* – drove them to the grange,

dipped them, sheared them.
All along Mastiles Lane bells rang

as pack ponies strained
under the weight of fleeces.

Only the wind with its empty cry
closes the gap between centuries.

a sheep counting rhyme used by shepherds in Northern England

Peak District
Derbyshire

Naming

St Edmund's Church, Castleton

A dog-eared pamphlet notes
the Norman chancel arch, the loss
of lancet windows.

Plain black box pews lack interest
until names carved on the panels startle me.

I whisper, *Samuel Cryer 1661,*
Thomas Cresswell 1662,

more confident, I begin to speak out loud –
Robert Hall 1663, John Hall 1676.

The echo of my voice
sweeps the rafters of the nave.

In every creak of the church's fabric,
in the loud tick of its clock,

in my footsteps on the hollow floor
I'm waking the dead.

Candle makers, lead miners, sheep farmers,
rope-makers from the huge cavern
in the Peak

pour through the church in procession
to share their lives

as if centuries were seconds
and they still had the power of speech.

Peak District
known as
'The Devil's Arse'
home of the last
'Troglodytes'
people who lived in
caves till 1915!

The Rope-Maker
Peak Cavern, Castleton

All day carrying rope
I walk the cold floor
forward back, forward back.

My home's a hut
in the depth of the rock.
My bed is straw.

Rain drips
from the mouth of the cave,
'Tis devil's touch, we say,

work harder.
I keep the woodpile stacked,
fetch water for porridge.

I won't walk death across the floor.

Winter months.
We walk faster to keep warm,
coughing in the smoky air.

There's no money
from visitors this time of year.
The coffin boat stands empty.

Icicles hang.
Peakshole water floods.
Devil's laughing now, we say

but I won't walk death across the floor.

Married to a miner
my sister lives in a strong stone house.

All her lads will work the lead,
will not make old men.

Better poor.
We'll walk forever
twisting hemp threads into rope.

Rope for sailors
up in the crow's nest,
rope for trucks down in the mines,

rope for pack men,
driving donkeys over the moor.
But I won't weave a hangman's noose

not for the commoners
fighting for their rights
not for the starving, forced to steal bread.

I'll never walk death across the floor.

walkers Edale, Derbys.
traditional route from
Castleton to Edale
'coffin road' old days
coffins were carried
to 'Hope Church'.

Over Hollins Cross

Deep in the hollow way
the path is a stream-bed.
Yellow mud splatters the stones.
It's a hard climb to Edale.
I would not do this alone,
not in the dark,
not when frozen mists
hover like dragons
above frosty grass.

Up ahead, guarded
by mist and distance
my companions grumble:
the price of flour,
the loss of the commons,
their looms left to rot.
I used to love the hand loom,
the rattle of the shuttle,
me mam singing.

My boot fills with water.
I can't see the potholes.
I'll have wet feet all day.
Old Jack at Spital Bridge says,
There's snow int' wind.
He can see it in the lead sky.
He can hear it
in the elm's twisting branches.
There'll be no path tonight.

Twelve hours in the mill
and we'll have to stay over,
knit black stockings
in exchange for shelter.
We can't use our pay.
It's Tommy notes now,
only accepted
in the master's stores.
His prices are high.

Dawn is coming;
I've dropped behind.
I glance over my shoulder.
Is the grey lady
from Castleton Hall following?
I quicken my pace
but want to turn to her,
see her candle flicker.
I want to take her hand and walk away.

Lead

Up early he is, straight down the mine
first thing – barely touches his porridge.
He's only thirty-two. I know he's slowing down.
That mine's crawling through his lungs
like a fat black beetle.
He should get out, start afresh, carrier perhaps.
You need a mint o' brass for a horse and cart.

I told him it was a no-good job.
You start with the lead, I said, *and that'll be it.*
You'll be dead by the time you're forty.
We need the money, he said. *Better the mine*
than starve. Do you want to watch
your children die? I said, *They'll die anyway*
if they work down Odin.

He'll end up like old Tom, can't work,
can't walk, can't eat. Tom was on his back
for eighteen months, arms like sticks,
face the colour of gritstone up on Kinder.
The mine done that. It's not worth it.
Not even for the black gold
as some calls it. I calls it devil's rock.

It'll do for my Jack. He will go on with it.
He's crazy. *Look at you,* I said,
you're no age and I've heard you cough.
Just a tickle, he answered. *I heard you coughing*
in the night, I said. He went out then,
slammed the door. George and Dragon, I'll bet.
What'll we do when he's gone?

Cumbria - Lake District

Honister Slate Mine

We run for the mine, escaping
a rain-soaked sky, a harsh landscape.
Little grows at the hause except slate.
Inside, in drained light, we hear
rain tattoo the thin roof.
We read notices and shiver.
Lives are resurrected in sepia photographs
docking with chisel and mallet –
riving, as slate is split down the grain,
dressing as it's shaped into roof tiles.
Old men in grimed trousers and work-boots
spent rigid-hours leaning into the task.
Ten minutes with the slate dust
in this bleak shed and we start coughing.

Village Scene
1348

A wick burns in an empty house,
the flame thin and faint in daylight.
The hearth is full of soft grey ash.

A man stands in a deserted street
arms limp at his sides, face pinched white.
A wick burns in his empty house.

He sees wind breathe life through beech leaves.
The wind can't help him. He's given up the fight.
His hearth is full of soft grey ash.

With aching limbs he struggles to his beasts,
unties their halters, sets them free.
A wick burns in the empty house.

There's the green barley he planted in spring.
He'll not reap it. The fever's at its height;
his hearth is cold with soft grey ash.

Evening shadows creep across the graves.
Prayers won't work. The priest was first to die.
A wick still burns. Back in his empty house

a man kneels beside a heap of sticks
without the will to light his fire.
A wick burns in the empty house;
his heart is full of soft grey ash.

Going In

Trebah Garden – January

I come expecting echoes,
a relentless tick, tick towards nothing
            and find a seal
carved from the trunk of a tree,
the flaps of his jaws curved into a smile,
long lines etched round his huge belly.

I come, my thoughts full of flu,
full of the dark
            winter mornings
to find droplets of white water
fluttering in the wind,
a fountain singing
over bronze gunnera leaves.

I come believing only
in dead things, bare branches,
dried leaves.
            Snug in the valley, tree ferns
make bright green umbrellas.
Higher up, palms with their hairy trunks
thrive in the wind.

What can a a flowerless, rain-washed
winter garden offer?
            Air fresh from the estuary,
children's laughter in the valley.
New Zealand flax called *cream delight,*
a zigzag path in the loud company of a stream.

I come hoping for nothing.
A notice board filled with photographs –
          segum, japonica, white lady,
iris, primula, Arizona sun –
          reminds me
the garden is waiting
to torch the valley with colour.

Snow Artist on Trewey Hill

Today I met a madman in the snow.
He stood beside his easel, feet in slush.
I asked him, *Why?* He said he didn't know.

Black sky, metallic sea, flakes driven in low.
In the ice-air breath is short. Lungs are crushed
today. I met a madman in the snow

who said he had to capture this, to tow
the landscape on to canvas with his brush.
I asked him, *Why?* He said he didn't know

what made him paint. I watched. His work was slow
as freezing fingers shook. I spoke. He whispered, *Hush!*
Today I met a madman. In the snow

he huddled in an overcoat, a strange crow
easing moors and cairns to life without rushing.
I asked him, *Why?* He said he didn't know.

With no answer I turned away to go
but took his image with me like a wish.
Today I met a madman in the snow.
I asked him, *Why?* He said he didn't know.

Epiphany at Pennance Farm

A metal-grey light flows from the Arctic
hail snow frost.

I climb slowly, feet too cold to feel
stones through my boots
past a brown pond, past black-plastic barrels of hay
stacked to cloud height.

A voice calls out from the barn.
I thread my way past machinery and sacks.
Megan, in her working clothes,

is surrounded by sheep bunched together
in the black straw, their faces framed
by grey wool clouds.

She tells me the ones with curly hair
are her own. *Do you lamb them?*
She smiles.

At night? How do you cope with college?
She shrugs. She's a farmer's daughter –
that's the way it is.

I remember dragging hay on sledges
through deep snow, feeding the ponies
after school

heaving water, humping tack, oiling hooves,
untangling tails, pulling up ragwort from the field –
the wet, sweaty stink of horse.

New life out of old dark stays with me
when I leave, a kick in my stride as I walk,
the metallic clouds glistening.

Trebah Garden – March

Not for the velvet of early primroses
          or the flush of pink
on a cultivated shrub I can't name –

not for the rich green of bluebell leaves
          promising
a woodland religion of colour –

I go to the garden for the hush
          of falling rain.

Beneath the thatched roof of Alice's Seat
I watch pages of water fill the valley,

          discover spring
still stored in my body within the book of rain.

Ceri Singing
The Tinner's Arms, Zennor

Ceri begins quietly
her voice gentle as water brushing reeds –
There is a house in New Orleans ...
I lean on the bar, something inside me taking ship.

The band has played all evening
with ringing tills, continual chatter,
children's cries
and a labrador who barked every few minutes.

How many times did my husband play
for a beer-swilling audience indifferent to jazz?

Ceri's voice rises
like wind through marram grass –
they call the Rising Sun ...

Caught in her rip tide
I'm swept to the front of the crowd,
wanting to hush the children,
gag the adults, drown the dog.

Ceri's voice bellies out like a ship's sail,
flooding the chattering –
It's been the ruin of many a poor girl.
Ah God I know I'm one ...

Background noise begins to ebb.
Even the dog is silent.
In this new country of sound all things are possible.

I remember my husband's band,
drunken laughter drowned
by the piercing beauty of the lead guitar.

Sanderlings on Marazion Beach

A wave ebbs.
They run towards the enormous Cornish ocean.

The next wave breaks. Miniature pistons, their legs
send them flat-out up the beach.

They can't be wild birds, can they?

More like pale Easter chicks
escaped from chocolate eggs.

Why do they pit themselves against the huge power of water?

The bird book tells me crustaceans and molluscs
rise to the surface in wet sand –
sanderlings can feed with short beaks.

That day wind drove us,
lifting the sand in clouds around our ankles.

We ran with it, hair in our eyes,
boots soaking as we splashed through puddles –

no book could tell us why.

Trebah Garden – Summer

Yesterday my son was in the garden.
He was beautiful in green,
but didn't speak.

I began to mutter,
Do you have a coat? A torch?
Will you be all right in the dark?

He turned away,
walked swiftly, past the gunnera
towards the sea.

Today I can't find him.
Death is hovering
in the cafe.

We talk about my son.
I look Death straight
in the hollows of his skull.

My son is in the garden
wearing green.
He's not ready. Let him be.

He's out of sight amongst the trees
but I know my son is in the garden
wearing green.

Going In

Rollers pound the beach.
                    Pebbles groan
as the sea slides back
into the next green mountain.

Why don't I admit I'm past it
                    stuck in the sand
like the rib of a wrecked ship
growing barnacles?

Am I like mum
                    after her final diagnosis?
She baked jam tarts for me, smiling –
See, I can still do this!

I imagine the smack
                    of the cold,
white horses beating through me,
a current dragging me in.

My daughter holds out her hand.
              I can't help but follow
leaping up as the waves tower,
altering their flow.

Coming out, my body burns
                    with wet salt health.
My hair is a tangle of mermaid's tresses,
my hands and feet are fins.

Winter Pass

The Grey Mare's Waterfall
Kinlochleven

Discovered late evening
          the fall
is the colour of a woman's hair

as she strides
          her last few years.

This sheer beauty
          offers no pulling back

from the uninhibited
          plunge
down vertical rock

a snatching of time,
          hurling it
into the pool.

If seconds were iron bars
          she could jam
in the cog wheels of a mill

she could not keep them
          against this grey fall.

Better to turn away
          climb
one slow, hard step

after another towards
          the winter pass
at Lairigmor.

Ulva

In a bay full of ghosts
          sit on a stub of lava.
Let your feet down into the loch,
watch them turn white.

Out there, coming in fast,
          are the longships.
Oars creak. Someone is shouting
in a language you don't understand.

The sea washes into crevices,
          swinging your feet forward,
pushing them back. Behind you
voices from the dun are screaming.

Children running,
          women dragging
cattle over peat hags.
It's too far to the mountain.

The local men gather,
          their spears raised,
ready and unready
for swords and helmets.

No worship of red deer,
          no prayer at the stones
can change this. Survival is a spear thrust
faster than a fish swims.

The bay is full of longships,
their captains the new kings.

Ulva – a small island off the west coast of Mull

Finding Dunadd

We come as our ancestors did,
searching for the causeway
through raised peat, the weight
of rucksacks grinding our shoulders.

The old track is blind to the road
where visitors let scenery slip by.
At night I dream of the sixth century,
my own smudged like a wood in mist.

In the car park we edge round tourists
in sandals and light dresses.
Toughened by the walk,
we climb easily up to the fort.

On the hill, wind from another century
drives away midges, lets us eat.
Sitting beside St Columba in a waking dream
I watch ships sailing in to land like birds.

Dunadd – hill fort in Argyll 500 to 1000 AD

When The Lamp Oil was Spilt

I was stripped, would have been beaten
until flesh fell from my back
and life ebbed.

Instead the stranger came, a holy man in brown robes
who grasped the arm of the soldier
holding the whip.

A whisper went round, *Columcille, Columcille.*
This man was no dove. *Let her speak,* he said.
Fear filled my mouth with grit.

I spilled lamp oil and my Lord fell, I whispered.
Deliberately, he asked?
No. I shook my head.

Lord Áedán glared. Warriors waited
sword arms ready. Wolf-silence hung
in the light of burning rushes.

His face lit by the rising moon, Columcille
gave Áedán look for look. *An accident.*
In the name of Christ have mercy.

Áedán shrugged,
and turned away. At his nod
the soldier dropped my wrist.

I fled to where the moon's silver
lay on the water, wishing I could thank this warrior
who fought without shield or spear.

Life returned: wood gathering, water fetching,
watching the forest patterns grow
on my mistress's loom.

That spring we journeyed to Iona
for the king-making. Serving my mistress
quiet as an otter in the loch,

keeping to the moon-shadow
I watched the Dove
make Áedán king.

St Columba (Columcille), inaugurated Áedán in 574 as king of Dalriada.

Prayer to St Columba

Friend of the weak   healer of the sick
this March stream is melted snow   filled with light
It brings me to you   I remember
you asked only   for the smallest door to paradise

I'm a wild woman   heather in my hair
goat-faced   elongated arms   web-footed
I belong to the distant lands   no one can visit
places unimagined   beyond the bestiary

comforter of the bereaved   when I lean
away from the emptiness   of rain   sea   rock
I lean to you   You smile from spring violets
from stitchwort   campion   wood anemone

God's companion   sometimes I long to make your journey
but mine is different   I worship the wild places
off-shore islands   mountains   lochs
where the sea eagles soar   where the red deer graze

Outcast

After reading 'The Banished Wife's Lament' from *The Exeter Book*

Men gather in the hall, my lord among them.
Tense faces are webbed with shadows
as the firelight leaps and sinks ...

What's to be done?
The serpent rules our fields,
steals from our barns, murders our children.

Answers are flung from man to man,
fall and perish at our leader's feet.

We must leave, he says, *seek new land*
untroubled by this beast.
Someone must sail ahead ...

I see the direction of his gaze. I'm afraid.
My lord steps forward, bends his knee,
expression drained from his dear face.

He'll sail along the coasts of an unknown land
where poets sing of whirlpools, dragons,
rocks like needles beneath the waves
where women with fish tails
comb their hair and beckon.

I run, try to hold him safe.
Please, we are newly come together,
have yet no children.

In the hall a woman
is less than a spindle thread.
Disapproval hangs
like an arrow in mid-flight.
My disloyal sisters pull back.

Now frost in the wild forest stiffens the grass.
My small heap of roots and nuts
can't sustain me,

but I care only for news of my lord.
No one brings it. I pace the cave, can't rest.
Oak galls, rotten bark, dead leaves refuse to speak.

On Loch Bá
Isle of Mull

Black-headed gulls gather for flight.

Curlews follow, flying the arc-echo
of their long curved beaks.

A heron rises slowly from the reeds.

I pick my way over pathless ground
where mallards rustle the lake edge with their chicks.

Unruffled by my presence
they slip into smooth black water.

Have they even seen me
as they swim the loch's long beauty?

They merge with the dark until
too far out for my vision – it's not them but me

fading into night.

Soulies Bothy

Here, the cuckoo calls all night,
her voice magnified,
ricocheting against the sheer sides of mountains.

I'm up early, don't wash,
pull a saucepan of water
from the burn for tea.

Red-legged oystercatchers
search the shore line for mussels.
I crunch the blue ovals

of empty shells in my sandals.
My boots are soaked.
I rub bog myrtle into my hands against midges,

stand close to the fallow deer
with their white duster bottoms.
Baby frogs jump on my bare toes.

Facilities are a long-handled spade. Mistakes are off limits.
I step gingerly over sphagnum moss
concealing nothing but water, mud and empty space.

We've had to walk in. We'll have to walk out.
Three days carrying tents, dried food, a medical kit.
Bridges are broken, rivers too deep to ford.

Here, the cuckoo's voice, louder than the siren
of an ambulance, keeps me brilliantly awake
through the Gaelic night's long dawn.

In Sanctuary

How many times have I lit a candle for you?
Twice on Iona,
            once in a low corner of the church
where candles already burned
and all around an ocean cried.

Not enough. I lit another in the chapel
before I left.
            It flickered in the draft
among rough stones. No more comfort there
than when Columba stood on the wind-scraped shore.

At each crisis I lit a candle,
remembering a friend
            who lit candles for all of us.
Yours burned brighter, lasted longer
than ours. Years passed. I was calmer.

I lit a candle in Exeter cathedral
but didn't know
            whether *happily ever after* was true
or I'd learned not to care. My hand still shook,
but I lifted you to the top of the stand.

Oban Night

Clear night. A paddle boat steams
            gently into the glass bay.
I hold the railings,

feel them give
            as my dad leans beside me,
breathing in quiet sighs.

He watches the mountains darken,
            longing to walk with me,
two wild shadows in a wilder landscape.

Instead I pace the streets
            at the start of my holiday,
all my time running ahead.

My dad follows, walking
            without arthritis in his knee,
his voice freed from stuttering.

He recalls his first air-force posting,
            his pay stopped
to cover the cost of his uniform.

Flying boats, the look-out post on Pulpit Hill,
and as we near a bare recreation ground
            I see him clear as light

winning the discus, the shot, tossing a caber.
            A twelve pound prize opened a social life.
He could afford a drink in the officers' mess.

I want to stay here with him,
            our shadows joined
dark to dark beneath the stars,

but it's time to find the guest house.
When I ring the doorbell
my dad steps back.

In a room full of cushions and frills
I'm alone with a bedside clock
ticking in the silence.

Saying Goodbye

Whitehorse Hill Burial

I

Long ago now.
I've watched the sun arc south
more times than I can remember

since she's gone. Her hair
a flame of sunlight, her laughter
the almond taste of meadowsweet.

Daughter of our spear-leader
all seven of our amber beads
were buried with her – our hopes

gone to ground as the fox
to his lair, the badger to his sett.
Lost as she was lost to us.

Was it right what we did?
It was a cold summer,
our sheep thin and the lambs crying,

the blackberries poor,
the hazelnuts rotten.
We couldn't grind them into flour.

By the ninth moon there was frost.
Wolves harried the sheep,
stalked the village edges.

How the whisper was started
I don't know – Vigi of the adder tongue
perhaps. It grew like a boil

swelling and bursting,
flooding the tribe.
They rose, spears ready.

Never while I draw breath,
was torn from our leader.
His daughter came from the priest's hut,

moonlight drenching her in silver
He has told me, she said,
it will be soon, when the moon is full.

I turned to seek my own spear –
to begin the long trek out.
If I'd stayed, I'd have killed the priest.

I could not let her go alone beyond the sun.
She must take the summer with her
in bunches of meadowsweet.

II

I dropped down into the forest
rain beating on my face

while wind howled
bending the ash branches

and the river ran high, fast –
full of white water.

My head ached with it.
My breath turned white.

The river beat over rapids,
its roar filling the valley.

I untied my holed stone.
I'd had it since I could crawl.

This, I whispered, stroking it.
Take this. Please let me pass.

The stone clung to my palm.
I bit my lip, threw it,

watched the current close over it.
The goddess accepted my gift –

beyond the bend she widened
and slowed. I waded across,

followed her bank until the storm died
and sunlight drew me towards the meadows.

Half-hidden in the reeds and long grass,
battered by the storm

were the last blooms
of meadowsweet.

III

Meadowsweet
soft as summer fruit

welcome
as the first violets
when winter unclenches its fist.

Our Lady of the Meadow –
as amber was our luck
she was our peace.

IV

Last year we picked stem after red stem
for our spear leader when a wolf tore his leg.

That autumn there was barely enough.
I took every flower I could find

until the sky darkened and the moon rose,
a perfect circle of bright, hard light.

V

I plunged uphill through the forest
not bothering to disguise my tracks.
At the steading they were piling dry hazel
on to the oak logs.

They brought our new goddess out
under the moon's black light
I tried to run to her, give her the meadowsweet
but they held me back.

Then – I cannot tell you – the words stick
in my throat like globules of bear fat.

The priest held the knife.
She died as the deer does, swift, quiet –
as I killed my own Grim when he broke his back.
I held him, fur to skin, but she lay
alone on the reed matting –
we were forbidden to touch.

We lifted her on to the pyre.
Her father set the torch to the kindling.

The yellow flower of the fire
still flickered in the dawn.
Her father's hands were the first to rake the hot ash,

skin peeling from his fingers.
We all searched
found as much of her as we could.

We waited. Three days I think, perhaps four
until everything was ready,
then set off before the dawn.
to Marghgwynn hill.
She would watch our steading.
She would see the forest and the estuary.
I carried the white flames of the meadowsweet.

That day it seemed we had broken out
from a cage of rain and wind.
The sun god was fierce,
his heat gnawing our skin. Vigi was jubilant.
We've done it, he said.
No one answered him.
We wrapped her in a bear pelt
with her bag, her earrings, her bracelet of tin
and placed her in the cist.
Over her tiny bones
I scattered the meadowsweet.

VI

afterwards
nothing
the weather did change

there were no more summers
weeping
from the third moon to the ninth

we wept her father
the tribe
we watched the sun god grow

and dwindle
          many times
but never did the summer

return to our hearts

This poem is based on the recent discovery of a cremation burial in a cist. It was the first discovery on Dartmoor of a burial with finds including a bag, bracelet, beads and the pollen grains of meadowsweet.

Ted Hughes OM
1930 – 1998

Dartmoor folds me in a wild bear-hug of heat.
Sheep lie on the bog in their heavy wool
or pant in mouse-sized shade.

I follow the ridge, Hound Tor, Wild Tor,
down to Knack Mine and stop to cool my feet
but the Taw runs hot over the stones.

I grew up with *October is a marigold,*
puzzled my way through
this *midnight moment's forest.*

White scars of army tracks
drag me towards the burning distance.
I struggle through ankle-twisting grass

to reach an island in the bog,
an open air church, a place of pilgrimage.
I collapse on a long, rounded, friendly stone.

I know *Elmet,* land and page –
have lived through *Season's Songs,*
breathing in *a faint sky-roar* of starlings.

Is it wrong to sit on him?
This is no tablet unveiled in the Abbey.
It's kindred to the tors –

like a park bench
erected in an old man's memory
it links the poet to a loved place.

I still catch my breath on
such a sodden raw-stone cramp of refuge
but have my own memories of Top Withins.

In the emptiness of the moor
sky is rinsed of cloud.
Whispering grasses barely touch the silence.

Quotations from *The Hawk in the Rain, Season's Songs* and *Birthday Letters.*

Gibbet

Blackdown Hill

Climbing uphill under a hot March sun
grass crackles under our feet.
Our shadows flow ahead over rough ground

towing us along. Mine is bent,
burdened.
This is not my shadow. It's a man's.

Sweaty heat, a long hard struggle
with damp clothes sticking to us.
His last journey. I won't make it mine.

How has he come to this?
Stealing a rabbit
to feed his wife and children –

or has he taken a life?
Our shadow pauses
is urged on. Is he innocent?

I can't continue to the top.
I call out to my friend,
It's late. We must get back. It'll get dark.

We turn down to the village.
My shadow is back
walking upright beside me

but as light fades it lengthens
as though it still clings to the hill
and will not leave his side.

How to Make a Dress Out of Stars

You need a clear sky   no moon
            or maybe the thinnest crescent
Go out on to the lawn   stand
with your back to the town   Listen

to the night murmur of waves
            letting them drown
chatter   traffic   Now
is the moment for separation

Remember to pick your stars
            like flowers
from where the Milky Way is thickest
Even stars are not forever

Go for variety   crimson   gold   silver
            Do not spill them
Shake them gently on to the table
their fall   your future

You need not be a seamstress
            skilful with thimble
or swift with a needle   Examine
each star   minutely

You are ready   Join them
            into your chosen pattern
a dress radiating light
as you step out

into the forest of the dark

Playing Alice

At home   my long-time-ago home
replaying the same scene
          again and again in my head

I can't forget a convex looking-glass
stretching my face   sideways
          playing games with size and shape

          Furniture belonged
not to the sitting room
          but to the Red Queen's domain

Surrounded by a heavy gilt frame
          the mirror hung
above the piano   To touch it

I climbed like a steeplejack
          balancing
on the red carpet piano-seat

and with one foot on the closed lid
          of the keyboard

squeezed myself into the space
between piano top and low-beamed ceiling

where   longing to escape
          my mother's voice
I breathed on the glass

watched it mist over and soften
          until I believed
I could push the flat palm of my eager hand

through it and slide
          without resistance
into Looking Glass House

Now I stand on the opposite side
          wanting to climb back
from Humpty Dumpty   the White Knight

a shop-keeper sheep knitting
          with eighteen pairs of needles

to descend from the piano
          back to the sitting room
where my mother is waiting

Twenty Fourth of November
for my mother

A wet, cold afternoon,
grey streets hooded with cloud.
Your birthday. I wanted to remember you.

I saw a church,
imagined sitting silently
watching the Virgin nurse her child.

It was shut. I went back to the high street,
everything unresolved.
Your sharp tongue hurt me, your spending,

but you loved to give presents –
a wind-up pink bear bounced across the table,
my children holding their sides with laughter.

You bought them coloured beads,
pottery cats, hand-crocheted gloves –
every knick-knack.

As I search for early Christmas presents
you nudge my elbow
pointing out a clock with a Gruffalo face.

We walk arm in arm surrounded
by tiny penguins wearing woolly hats,
mugs with yellow sheep cavorting round their rims

and I begin to understand
all the conjugations of the verb
to forgive.

To My Grandmother

If I could tell you how beautiful
the rowan is this year, its first serrated leaves a milky green,
silver patches on its mottled trunk –
if I could tell you
how the rough edges of the garden are full
of yellow poppies, speedwell –

perhaps you know these things –
you knew the child I was,
running through ling in the Punch Bowl
while you walked white sand paths
with a friend saying, *She's a good walker.*
She only gets tired on the road.

Somewhere in my teens I left you
as if you were a toy I'd out-grown.
One morning before my parents were awake
I answered the phone.
A hospital nurse spoke kindly.
If I could have stopped time then ...

I was young, went on alone.
Sometimes I paused to say, *I did this, I achieved that*
or tried to share my travelling with you –
the way the swallows gathered on the lawn,
the first primrose in a spring lane.
You never answered, not a sentence or a word.

Now I travel backwards, searching for you.
Your ancestors were broom squires in the Bowl.
Your name is always dancing through my thoughts –
Millicent Eva Lawrence.
I hold it, cupped in my hand
as I try to piece you together.

Near Hartington

She lives away now.
Grown up long ago.
When we chat we tread water.

We visit Dove Dale,
lose the path, a boggy field –
she only has her trainers –

but the river dances
between limestone cliffs

and a grey heron breaks
from under our feet
rising upwards
in deep slow wing-beats.

I've never seen a heron, she says.
Look how his neck's drawn in.

I stop floundering,
move from the edge of her

to stand as if we were one person in one place.

Saying Goodbye

We still have a whole day's walk ahead –
leaving Alfriston
to cross the tiny Cuckmere,

climb through oak woods at Westdean,
gaze down
on the river's sweeping meanders,

pant up and down the switchback
of the Seven Sisters
under a fierce sun. I stagger

to the final South Downs marker,
cling to it for support
as a kind passer-by takes our photograph.

On the beach, our feet too hot and sore
to walk barefoot over pebbles,
we crawl to the sea, giggling.

The rain starts at five o'clock
almost to the minute
as predicted by your iPhone.

Our train rushes too fast
through back-to-back towns
in a blur of cloud and concrete.

In Brighton our journeys divide.
I hug you. *Goodbye. Take care.*
Don't walk through Nunhead cemetery in the dark,

as if you're still ten, while you
satisfy yourself I'm boarding
the correct train.

Indigo Dreams Publishing Ltd
24, Forest Houses
Cookworthy Moor
Halwill
Beaworthy
Devon
EX21 5UU
www.indigodreams.co.uk